India Travel Survi

By Shara Sharma

MW01295456

Table of contents

Introduction

With news of rapes in India hitting the headlines all over the world, there has been a decline in tourists visiting India, especially by those women who travel alone. But to be honest, India is not the worst destination for female tourists but at the same time, we cannot say that it's the safest either. Many female tourists have travelled safely in remote places of India all alone and have felt safe. However due to the recent incidences of rape and harassment, female tourists to India are not feeling safe anymore, especially if they are travelling on their own. The danger is not just of rape or murder; the occurrence of other crimes like being duped, taken undue advantage of, groped/touched or subjected to eve teasing is also very common. Not to mention that travelling to India for the first time can be a culture shock to some.

Foreigners really need to understand the country before they travel and take precautions so that they can feel confident and be safe in India. For example, women touring India from Western nations have to realise that they cannot go swimming everywhere in their bikini, enjoy late night discos or travel with the drivers sitting in the front seat of auto rickshaws. The country is not yet ready for that sort of revolutionary freedom.

Most of the female tourists, especially those who are travelling alone have complained about being rudely stared at, groped in buses, trains and crowded places and stalked by men. Travelling alone, without a male companion can be like signalling for unwanted advances from men. Often lewd remarks are passed at them, followed by cat-calls and eve teasing which can be terrifying. Scams are also common as newcomers to India are not familiar with the tricks of the cheats.

Incidences of rape have been on the rise in India or at least there has been a rise in reporting of cases in the country by the victims. Though, most of the victims are local females, the risk to foreigners touring India is also there. Delhi seems to be winning the competition as the most unsafe city of India for women. Some of the recent attacks on foreign tourists have been a shameful blot on the policy of Indians who revere the guests at home or country by saying 'Atithi devo bhavah' meaning guests are equal to Gods. Sometimes I just wonder how hypocritical we can be!

Here are some of the cases in recent times against foreign tourists in India:

The attack and molestation of a 16 year old Swedish girl by New Year revellers in Kochi (Kerala).

Gang rape of a Swiss woman when she and her husband camped in a forest area of the central Indian state of Madhya Pradesh.

The rape of a German scholar by a son of a top Indian police officer.

Attack on a British national, who fortunately escaped by jumping out of her window in Agra (the city of the Taj Mahal).

Rape of a tourist from South Korea who was drugged and raped in Madhya Pradesh by the son of the owner of the hotel she was staying in.

The rape and killing of 15 year old Scarlett Keeling from Britain on the Anjuna beach in Goa.

Rape of two Australian girls in Jaipur, who did not receive any help from the police department upon complaining.

This is just the tip of an iceberg. The attacks in India are not targeted only at foreign female tourists, its worse for local women - for instance, the brutal gang-rape of Jyoti Singh Pandey on a moving a bus in Delhi that resulted in her death was a wakeup call for Indians. Though she was not a foreigner, her rape spread fear among the tourists due to the brutality of the incidence not to mention that it took place in the heart of the Indian capital.

Indian men have a lot of misconceptions about western women especially white women who they consider promiscuous and who do not take sexual relationship very seriously. Added to this, is the great desire of Indian men for fair skinned women.

There has been no statistics to prove a completely planned crime against foreigners in India, but it does happen. Indian tourism department has been concentrating on attracting tourists to India with their 'Incredible India' campaigns, while ignoring the safety of tourists to India. Indian tourism department needs to improve on their tourism marketing strategy by bringing in more updated safety procedures which should make foreigners feel safe in India rather than showing off attractive tourist destinations.

It is quite normal to be apprehensive while travelling to India for the first time especially if you have heard stories about rapes, climate, traffic, population and so on. As you step out of the airport you'll notice more people than anywhere else in the world. It is like a sea of people all around, for someone coming from the west it would definitely come as bit of a shock.

"It's like being in a video game. I don't know which way to look. It's a bit chaotic, but there's an underlying calm, a flow, that you all seem to understand. India is a paradox" is what Oprah Winfrey had to say about India.

Crowded streets, a sea of people, crammed full buses, and trains is often the picture that comes to one's mind about India. But there is a joy and excitement in this madness which is an experience which you may savour only in this amazing country.

Chaos and India are synonymous in a sense. For example, a drive can be a spine-tingling experience. It's not that India isn't much of a pedestrian friendly country; there is no system or facilities in place which give priority for those on foot. The trick here is to follow the crowd. So yes, there will be confusion, disarray and sometimes even mayhem but it's all part of the 'Indian experience'. It may take you some time to adjust to such a contrast in terms of ways of life or even the way 'life functions' in this part of the world but rest assured at the end of it all you will start feeling connected to this place. It is just impossible to stay untouched by its charisma - slightly wayward yes, but definitely not one to be ignored.

I have tried to cover most of the safety issues foreign women face in India and have tried to explain how to deal with it. I have also included some practical guides to common issues faced by tourists in India. There is no need to fear India, all you need to do is take some precautionary steps, be aware of the culture, do certain things, wear certain clothes and use common sense and I am sure you will be fine. I hope this book would be of use to those women planning on visiting India.

Chapter 1: Inhuman treatment of women in India

Many people would be shocked to know that India in the past was a matriarchal society, which means that the society gave rights to its women to be the head of the family. Some communities in states of Karnataka, Kerala, Maharashtra and Bengal still follow matriarchal status where families are ruled by the oldest living woman. In addition, Indians have worshipped thousands of Goddesses. It is believed by the Hindus that the Goddess Shakti was the power that created the universe. Women belonging to upper class were given rights to choose their husbands in a matrimonial ceremony called the "swayamvara" (practice of choosing a husband), where the men had to prove themselves worthy of winning the woman's hand.

However over a period of time, the condition of women changed in India - the worst during the medieval period, when widow remarriage was prohibited, "sati" (immolating on the husband's funeral pyre) and "jauhar" (Rajput Hindu tradition of honorary self immolation) was prevalent, child marriage was legalised, and women were exploited and mistreated in every walks of life.

In modern times, Indian women have proved their mettle time and time again. Women had bravely fought against the British for the freedom of India but when India got its freedom, unfortunately women continued to remain in chains metaphorically speaking. Even to this day, freedom to do what they want has not been fully granted to women of India by society. However, when given opportunities, Indian women have demonstrated their excellence in sports, politics, science, arts and bringing fame to India. Yet, the society continues to remain backward reducing the place of the girl-child between the four walls of her home to make babies and look after the family.

India is a country which has seen the longest rule by a woman prime minister in the world, a record set by Indira Gandhi. The country has seen great achievements from women like Savitribai Phule (social reformer), P.T.Usha (athlete), Bachendri Pal (first Indian woman to climb Mount Everest), Indra Nooyi (Indian-American business executive), Lata Mangeshkar (Award winning play-back singer) and many others. Unfortunately despite everything, the condition of women in the country is a shame - rocked by crime against women in every form.

Though under the law and Indian constitution, the women of India enjoy lot of benefits but in reality they are exploited, victimised, subdued, tortured and humiliated in every walk of life. The benefits have so far remained on paper and have not reached the ordinary women who suffer various kinds of violence and exploitation.

Although India has come out of the medieval times where ills such as Sati (widows killing themselves on the funeral pyre of their dead husbands) and devadasi system (girl married to a deity and made to work for the temple all her life) were outlawed due to great reforms which took place in the 19th century; crimes like dowry deaths, rapes, female infanticide, inequality of rights, domestic violence, marital rape and other such offenses against women still exist. Even the great reformers have failed so far to bring about a change in the society.

The girls from economically poor background often are married at very young ages, a time when they are physically and mentally not prepared to bear the burden of marital life. Sadly, some of these girls are below the age of 15 years, a time when they are supposed to enjoy their childhood and get an education. The nuisance of dowry has led to some people opting for female infanticide that has resulted in an imbalance in male-female sex ratio of India. Many couples are not only resorting to aborting the female fetus but also killing the girl child during infancy. The males are outnumbering females in many Indian states due to these selective abortions. It is thought that in some places of India, there are about 1000 males to every 800 females.

The life of some women is so grim that economically they are dependent on their fathers before marriage, husbands after marriage and sons in old age. There is a lot of imbalance in the male/female interpersonal relationship creating male dominance in the process. Though man is considered to be the earning member of the family, the work done by the woman in rural India surpasses that of men. But unfortunately, they do not get recognition or appreciation for this as it is considered to be their duty - to work and care for their family. They have no rights to speak in family matters or important decisions.

On the contrary; boys get better food, clothes and education compared to their sisters. They usually grow up enjoying their childhood, whereas the girls are made to bear the burden of domestic responsibility at a very young age. Girls often suffer from malnutrition, anemia and fail to reach their full potential growth. Although it has improved in recent years, the literacy rate for women in India remains at 54% whereas the literacy rate for men is 76%.

Divorced women in many parts of the country are looked down upon. Women therefore try to save their marriages despite the hardship. This causes them to remain with their abusive husbands and continue to bear hardships, domestic violence and brutality. Some women fear that if they leave, they may have to suffer at the hands of others. Since there are no safety nets for women, they continue to suffer.

How can we expect development and progress in India when women are oppressed? The prosperous future of India lies with the progress and development of its women. It is now time for another freedom movement in India where the women will be freed from the chains of society and share equal rights with men.

No wonder due to this dominating attitude of Indian men; they try to suppress, subdue, harass and weigh female visitors to India in the same way they do to their women in India.

Chapter 2: Rape in India

Indians who were at one time offended by the reference of India as the 'country of snake charmers' would be glad to hear that now due to the recent developments, it is now being referred to as the 'country with rapes'.

When you pick up a daily newspaper in India, you are bound to read about occurrences of rapes. The victims are from all walks of life, they could be a domestic servant, school or college girl, widow, working woman, mother of 5 kids or an elderly person. The age of the rape victims have varied between 3 – 55 years, though there have been more extremes on rare occasions. The scary fact is that, these reports are just a small fragment of what is going on, as many of the rape cases go unreported hidden in the psyche of the victim tormenting her for life. If the victims belong to tribal or minority groups, then the reports are even lower. Even when reported, the conviction rate is as low as 26% in the country, which in turn has further encouraged the rapists to commit these crimes knowing fully well that their chances of being prosecuted is slim.

India being a highly patriarchal society, rape is not just about sex but also about male domination, violence, power and ego. The northern part of India is more male dominated than the south. The men are brought up making them feel that women are for their dominance and service. They usually command total submissiveness from the women in the house be it sister, sister-in law and even the mother. When these men make sexual advances towards a woman outside the house, they take it as a personal insult to their male chauvinistic ego if the woman resists. More often, they rape women to prove their authority, dominance, power and as a punishment. Rape is also committed as a form of revenge in family disputes.

In most cases of rape, the girl is often blamed. The family and the raped girl may not even lodge a complaint with the police fearing social out-casting. This further encourages the rapists, who feel assured that they can get away with rape. Even if the girl dares to go against the society and lodge a case with the police station, there is no assurance that she will get justice. In some horrible instances of police inefficiency; the victim has been harassed, molested and abused by the police. The dress code and conduct of the raped woman is often questioned, and she is often blamed for what happened. Very often, we hear the phrase "she invited it" and what was "she doing late at night" or "she shouldn't have been there".

High value is placed on the virginity of the girl and the social system looks down upon girls who have males in their friends group especially in rural India. Most of the Indian men have been brought up in a setup where they have interacted only with other men. They often do not have any platonic friendships with females. Neither are Indians comfortable communicating with unknown members of the opposite sex. The lack of interaction between the two sexes has given rise to deprived men viewing every woman as a potential sex object. Most of the Indian men are either too shy or get excited when they have to interact with females.

Subject of sex is still considered to be a taboo in many regions of India and people hesitate to discuss it. Schools are yet to come up with sex education and parents do not talk about sex with their children. With the advent of internet on mobile phones, porn sites have been their 'informative friends' for many. In addition to this, pornographic materials are freely available in the market. In a disclosure, a newspaper on 9th of July 2013 reported that CCTV cameras installed in Delhi's Metro trains have been used to capture intimate moments of couples and the video footages have even been uploaded on pornographic sites.

The whole thing has created wrong ideas about love, sex, sexuality, penetration, prostitution and negative perception about women. Some even believe what they see in pornography can be done in real life. The overexposure to porn magazines and websites disturbs the minds of the youth who look for opportunities to vent out their disturbed feelings. Without proper rape laws and inability of the administration to punish the rapists, causes more rape of innocent victims.

Marital rape is common among poor sections of Indian society since a lot of girls are married at very young ages. Education, employment and giving more rights to women will remove the rape culture from its root. Law should be stricter and harsher punishments should be given even for small offences against women. The Indian society has to give equal rights to their women and empower them.

The brutal rape of a young woman in a moving bus in the capital city of India has seen a wave of protests arising all over the country. This has created awareness in the general public. The gang-rape led to the formation of an anti-rape law, the Criminal Law (Amendment) Bill-2013, giving life sentences and even death sentences for rapists along with harassment punishment for offences like acid attacks, stalking and voyeurism.

But honestly, the law will not succeed against a patriarchal and misogynistic culture which is prevalent in India; therefore the system has to be cleaned from within. May be India will see a change soon.

Chapter 3: Is India safe for women travelling alone

Over the past few years, if there is one country that has garnered more attention than any other when it comes to female tourists - it is India. This particular country is one of the few countries around the world where female tourists are urged to stay away from. I want to take a little look at whether these claims are true, which of course will give you the answer if India is safe for female tourists or not?

Well, firstly let me be clear on one thing. No country is truly safe for female tourists - not by a long shot. However, most countries of the world can be travelled safely provided they have the knowhow to stay safe. Perhaps one of the main reasons why India has earned a negative reputation as of late is because there are plenty of news articles and personal experiences out there detailing harassment of women across the country. This is of course bad but what you may not know is that countries such as Sweden have far more rapes in the country than India. The only real reason as to why this country gets a negative reputation is because the governments of various countries are more likely to give warnings about India than European countries.

Most people are going to suggest that you only travel with a male. There are a lot of men that seem very 'hands on' when it comes to women who are travelling on their own in India. No doubt, if you are with a man then you can eliminate most advances rather quickly and many women in fact prefer to travel this way but you can always travel with another female companion. But do remember, if you are on your own or with another woman or someone else, this does not mean that you will be safe. It will certainly be enough to make you feel comfortable and be a little safer.

So, is India safe for female tourists? Should females travel to Indian alone? Well, yes and no. As mentioned previously, most places around the world aren't truly safe. However, I believe that a female tourist should be safe in India provided she comes up with a fairly decent tour plan and know exactly what to do and where to go.

If you are travelling on your own then I suggest that you come up with a decent tour plan. Make sure that the tour planners are well known. Don't head out too late at night, and certainly give those long expanses of countryside a miss as this is where most of the danger is centered. Before you head out, you should also learn a few self defense tips I have included in this book to ensure that you don't suffer from too many problems, and if you do, you know how to deal with them. It's better to be safe than sorry.

Let's face it, like most places around the globe, India isn't really safe for a female tourist travelling on her own. However, if you stay near the cities, you should be fine, provided you use your own common sense, learn some of the local language, do not wear skimpy clothes and get to know the culture.

I understand the message is somewhat vague but it all depends on how you travel in India. It's all about planning well and being careful. Please read the rest of the chapters and pay particular attention to the tips and how to be safe in India.

Chapter 4: Rape and sexual assault of foreign women in India

The recent rape of a Swiss woman by 5 men generated huge publicity globally, threatening the tourism industry of India estimated at nearly $18 billion. The Swiss couple was cycling to Delhi on their way to Taj Mahal. After setting out from Orchha (Madhya Pradesh), they camped in a tent near a forest area where they were attacked by men armed with sticks. The couples were robbed, the woman gang-raped and her husband assaulted in the shameful attack.

In an immediate follow up, a British national Jessica Davies (31) of London was almost attacked in her hotel room. Fortunately she escaped with minor injuries by jumping through the window. A rickshaw driver who was passing by took her to a police station. The culprit was none other than the hotel manager of Hotel Agra Mahal who offered a free hair massage for the tourist and would not take 'NO' for an answer. This happened in Agra, a city that has pulled tourists like a magnet with the glory of the Taj Mahal is even more shocking. Since these incidents, there has been a lot of talk about crimes against foreign tourists in India especially of the sexual types.

Not all Indians try to molest or sexually attack foreigners. Many are very conscious about spreading the wrong message among foreigners about their own motherland, so behave extra good in their presence. When the Italian model Ginevra Leggeri was groped by a man in Mumbai, the city she visited for work, she slapped him and screamed for help. Two Indian men, who were travelling by motorbike, stopped and helped her by confronting the attacker. They then assured her safety. So you see that there are some opportunists lucking around and at the same time there are ordinary decent people who are willing to help out.

These incidences are enough to tarnish the image of India as a country where culture is supposed to show great hospitality to visitors. Statistically, India has very low rate of rapes, which stands at 2 for every 100,000 where as it is 30 per 10000 in the USA. However as mentioned earlier, this could be due to the fact that not all rapes in India are reported.

The worst part is that the rape and sexual assault against women touring India has been on the rise even in popular tourist spots frequented by visitors for decades. The most horrible statistics is that these rapists are not always uneducated or underprivileged but some of them are active politicians or are related to people holding responsible positions in India.

In one such incident in 1994, the grandson of the then chief minister of an Indian state, had allegedly abducted and molested Katia Darnand, a French national touring India. Another reprehensible incident is the rape of a German tourist in Alwar (in Rajasthan) who was assaulted by Biti Mohanty, the son of the senior police officer of Orissa state. Yet in another incident, a local politician of Goa was accused of raping a Russian tourist.

Other incident that sends shivers amongst foreign tourists is the case of a 35 year old tourist guide who allegedly raped a South Korean tourist near the tourist hotspot Manali. A party organiser who used to organise high profile parties in the National Capital Area of Delhi raped a Chinese citizen in Delhi's Hauz Khas area.

Many gullible tourists fall prey to sweet talking local men who pretend to ensure their safety. In the case of the Japanese woman who was gang-raped in Pushkar, it was due to misplaced trust in the hotel manager of Quiet Palace. He had taken money from the tourist for safe keeping, saying she could be robbed. Later he gave her a drink laced with drugs and raped her with three more accomplices.

In another incidence, two Japanese tourists were befriended by local lads called Raees and Sunny. Sunny who fluently spoke Japanese invited the victims to share a drink. Later these two men assaulted these women and kept them confined for three days. They were joined by another man later on. The Japanese women alleged that they were gang-raped by the men, who lured them into the hotel and gave them drinks that were spiked with sedatives.

British girl Scarlett Keeling (15) found dead on Goa's beach was suspected to be raped and murdered. Many British tourists have reported cases of molestation and sexual assault including at popular attraction such as Goa, Agra, Jaipur, Delhi, Mumbai, Kochi and Bangalore. This has led the FCO (foreign and commonwealth office of UK) to issue warnings to their citizens to respect the local dress code and customs, keep away from lonely places and to take extra precautions with their safety.

The Chinese government also has retorted strongly to rape of the Chinese women, while some European nations have also warned their citizens going to India about their safety. In addition, a lot of media coverage of rape incidents in India has caused concerns and anxiety amongst Australian women who plan to travel to India according to the Australian envoy in India.

This goes to prove that countries do not take it lightly when their citizens are treated badly in India. Therefore it is time for Indians to wake up and take measures to ensure safety of foreigners in India if tourism is to survive and flourish.

Chapter 5: How are white foreign women perceived in India

There was a case when a Romanian woman was travelling in a rickshaw and the driver stopped and attempted to grab her thigh. In another case, some Indian men were arrested for attempting to molest 2 young Canadian girls. In yet another disgusting case, a man raped a British girl after giving her a lift, a Swiss woman was gang-raped in Madhya Pradesh, and a British woman had to jump out of the hotel window when the hotel owner tried to get into her room at 4 in the morning. The list of such stories is endless. Don't you just wonder what exactly is going on?

The question that comes to mind is, why do Indian men behave badly with foreign white women? I have not heard of many African women being harassed in India. I think I might have the answer!

Foreign women are seen as women from the west who are used to having a lot of sex. Many Indian men consider foreign countries specially countries of Europe and America where sex is considered "open and free". Indian men are frustrated and sex as a topic is a taboo. Most Indian men have sex after marriage and it's natural for them to want sex. Indian men are virgins well past their twenties/thirties or till they get married. Some of them frequently visit prostitutes to cater for their physical demands.

Indian women do not visit countries alone and express their freedom by travelling. So, when they see foreign women travelling alone, they automatically tune in to the misconception that they must have come to India to have sex hence it's OK for them to make a move. In addition, the average Indian man is not used to the idea that a woman can do whatever she likes in the west. The hard truth is that women in India are not really respected in society as much as they are in the west.

Bollywood, the Indian film industry may have a part to play in all this. Many films show foreign white woman dancing in miniskirts with a glass of wine in her hand. This gives them the idea that foreign women are a fair play and interested in sex. In fact, the entire film industry is based on "sexy fair skinned women" dancing and singing. Perhaps these are some of the reasons why violence against white foreign women is on the increase.

Another point is that Indians are obsessed with the fair skin. Even when men look for wives they try to avoid dark skin women. White or fair skin is very appealing to Indian society. Basically, Indian men prefer fair-skinned women to darker ones and there is nothing fairer than white. If you don't trust me, then go on any Indian matrimonial site and see it for yourself. In addition, most Indian actresses in Hindi movies are fair skinned including those from South India (comparably darker than North Indians). In addition, there are lots of facial creams in the Indian market claiming to whiten the skin and they have doing great business.

Basics & Lifestyle

Age	27	Diet	Veg
Marital Status	Never Married	Drink	No
Height	(160cm)	Smoke	No
Complexion	Fair	Personal Values	Will tell you later
Body Type	Average	Sun Sign	Capricorn
Body Weight	Not Specified	Blood Group	Not Specified
Grew up in	India		

Furthermore, the use of skimpily dressed white cheerleaders in IPL cricket confirms that the way in which some Indians consider western women - which is misconceived notion that that they are more "ready" to do anything compared to Indian women. Whenever there is a "wicket or sixer", these mostly white cheerleaders would dance showing a lot of skin to the mostly conservative Indian audience again giving the impression that white women lack moral discipline. In fact, I find it extremely troubling and frightening to see some Indian men drooling on these foreign women.

The world of porn is full of pornographic material mostly showing men with white women having sex in almost every sexual position imaginable. In contrast, there are very few Indian porn sites and most of them have low quality material most often videos and photos made from hiring prostitutes. One really has to work hard to get quality Indian pornographic material. Again porn sites solidify the misconception that foreign women very are interested in sex. A very sad state of affairs but I am afraid this is very much what shapes the perspective of some Indian men.

It is virtually near impossible to mix with the opposite sex in India and hence many men do not know how to act when they see foreign women and end up with all weird and awkward activities around them. They get this wrong impression that white women are easy going unlike their Indian counterpart hence they are allowed to say or do anything they want. They are under the impression that western society is sexually liberated.

American movies often depict women having boyfriends or partners before marriage and having sex and losing their virginity. Now Indian men get this impression that they too can easily get white women in bed easily with the drop of the hat and all they need to do is just talk to her. This is why tourists are generally more vulnerable and men often think that they can get away with it if they were to do something to them.

The western world celebrates its freedom, and that is something Indians find hard to understand. But all in all, sexual harassment is everywhere. Imagine a woman passing by and being whistled at by construction workers somewhere in the Western world. Groping of women in the New York subway is nothing new. In fact a woman can have their bottom pinched anywhere in the world.

The sole plan of any male is to get the woman in bed but the behaviour of Indian men is less sophisticated and they end up staring, groping or raping the vulnerable tourists.

Finally it's all about fitting in the crowd, learning the local language, not wearing skimpy clothes that show bra straps or tight fitting clothes and learning some Hindi, not showing any signs of readiness of sex, not accepting food and drink and maintaining a safe distance.

Chapter 6: How to avoid being raped in India

When Ram Singh and his associates gang-raped Jyothi Pandey on the moving bus in Delhi, he told the other rapists not to worry as it can be handled. He cleaned the bus and they all carried on with their regular lives as though nothing would happen to them. The scariest part of rapes in India is the feeling instilled in offenders. They know it is easy to get around the system. The sixth offender, a juvenile just falling months short of 18 had raped the girl twice and is known to have tortured her the most. In fact, he took her guts out with his bare hands. Anyone under 18 is considered a juvenile and rarely given harsh punishment no matter what the crime. This proves the inability of Indian system in handling rape cases and convicting offenders.

So it is finally left up to the women to come up with strategies which could save them from being raped.

Here are some ways that could prevent rape:

Be confident

Encouraged by the system that has failed women miserably, rapists look for victims; preying on them, sending fear though their hearts and feeding on that fear to attack. The way to tackle their confidence is by acting 'confident' and carrying yourself with a purpose even if you are just strolling. Trusting your instincts, reflexes and voices at the first sign of attack can save you from rape. If you are being followed then take a proper look at the stalker. No one wants to be identified, therefore this discourages them.

Go with your gut instinct

Like in any place in the world, walking all alone in lonely places or in the dark can give the rapist the much sought after opportunity to rape. If you are uncomfortable with a place, person or food offered to you - go with your gut feeling and avoid them at any cost. Nothing is worth taking the risk.

Resist

If you are attacked by a single man, put up a fight. Either out up a passive or an active resistance whichever suits the situation. Passive resistance is where you need to think and work your way out of the situation. Whereas in active resistance you will need to startle the attacker with whatever you have at hand. Often rapists do not want to be identified, hurt, or waste time over their victim. If you put up a brave fight, they may not find you worth going after. But watch out for a group of men because they will definitely be able to empower you. If you are carrying a pepper spray, umbrella, heavy purse or something worth making an impact, use it relying on your instinct to attack.

Avoid close proximity with men

Riding the rickshaw or auto-rickshaw is a popular activity amongst the tourists and sometimes female tourists can make mistakes for instance sitting on the same seat as the driver. Indian women know that they shouldn't get on the seat with the driver. Indian men are not used to such close proximity with women. It does not take much time for them to get aroused when a female share the small seat with them. Women have to learn to keep their distance from men in India and not indulge in foolish activities like getting into the front seat with the driver.

Follow a dress code

We all agree, the victims do not invite rape by wearing certain dresses but can we really be sure? Sometimes the skimpy dresses can actually provoke these criminal minded men who are not used to seeing skin exposure in real life.

To be on the safer side, it is best to wear dresses that are accepted locally. This way, a tourist will not stand out of the crowd, but will blend well with the locals without attracting any unwanted attention. I know it sounds "subjective" but in a society like that of India's, we just cannot be too careful. This is not to say at all Indian men are mugs. Most of them are nice, but a few criminally minded individuals can spoil the fun. Should we really take our chances?

I have written a post on my blog that white women should wear the Kurta (also known as kurti) which is something like a shirt that goes up the knees. The Indian salwar kameez with a dupatta to cover the shape of the breast is also a good idea.

Do not rely on your companion

A lone man is no match for a bunch of rapists. However, both of you can be a deterrent to a single person with criminal intent on his mind. When a woman is attacked by a group of men, there is little a man escorting her can do to save her.

Hide your long tresses

Sometimes men look for victims with long hair which can be easily grabbed. If you are short haired then it's fine. However, if your hair is long then you could cover it with a scarf especially at places where you feel you may be targeted.

Avoid food and drinks from strangers

When strangers offer you food or drink, just think why they are being so generous to you in a country where large percent of people suffer from hunger. The drinks or food laced with drugs or intoxicants will render you helpless against their attack. Do not take any chances.

Do not trust

Do not fall prey to sweet talk of strangers who invite you to have a drink, offer lifts or show extra concern. They could just be wolves in sheep's clothing. If you are travelling in trains, it's paramount that you do not accept food or drink from no one. You never know that it could be spiked with drugs. Either take your own food or the food that is supplied by railway authorities. The food sold on the platform is generally okay however you have to remember that it could cause stomach upset.

Chapter 7: Travel tips for women in India

Indians have very strong feelings about their religion, culture and traditions which is not understood by foreigners. History has been witness to this ignorance in the past. The Indian Mutiny of 1857 is a good example of how the British could never have guessed that the greased cartridges (with pig and cow fat) would start a revolution that would end rule of the East India Company and fuel a desire for independence amongst the Indians finally ending colonial rule in India.

Keeping few tips in mind would ensure your safe touring of India:

What many female tourists do not realise is that in India, women do not enjoy equal status as men at least in practice. Though you may find men wearing skimpy clothing covering just their loins, skimpy clothes worn by women will get them in trouble.

Places of worship are not open to everyone in many places in India. In some places, women are prohibited, whereas in other places people belonging to other communities are not allowed.

Even when you are allowed inside a temple, be careful to take off the footwear before entering as it is considered to be an unforgiveable offence.

The pure vegetarians like some of the religious communities of Jains, Brahmins, Lingayats and other communities have strong dislike for non-vegetarians. In temples dedicated to their deities, even articles made of leather or hide will be considered as offensive. To be on safer side, it is better to avoid taking these articles inside religious places.

If you are with a partner, do not get too cosy or exhibit your affection freely in public. It will be considered offensive by many people, especially in rural areas although in the urban areas this is fine.

Do not give in to sob stories of beggars and other people who are trying to take advantage of you. By giving money to beggars, you will be encouraging them to harass more foreign tourists. There is a section on how to deal with beggars, please do read it.

If your fellow passenger is showing interest in you, offers to help you or offers something to consume, do not give in. Don't eat or drink anything from strangers. They could be trying to drug or spike you and take advantage of your intoxication afterwards.

Even if you are a woman, do not take photographs of Indian women without their permission.

A polite response, friendly gesture or a helping hand lent from your side could be misinterpreted as sexual advances from you by the opposite sex. Some Indian men have formed an image of western women to be more open about sex and some think that they are seeking pleasure by engaging with men.

Plan your tour with licensed travel agents who can make sure that your itinerary is well planned. They can also provide you with drivers/guides with good records and those who do not have criminal cases against them. Remember unlike the west, criminal records are rarely checked when hiring people. Good travel organisers will ensure that their employees do not have a criminal past.

The drivers of auto-rickshaws, taxis or manual rickshaws know that you are not familiar with local roads and routes. This will encourage them to take you to your destination by taking long routes to make more money. Worse thing is that they can take you to a lonely spot and rob or assault you. GPS on your mobile would help! Do not hesitate to disembark when you feel something is not right. For safety, you can always hire taxis or auto-rickshaws through the hotels or guesthouses you are staying with. Prepaid taxis and autos are also considered safer than general transport.

Wear Indian dresses such as "kurtis" or something which will cover you properly, even if you are uncomfortable in it. Some religious places make it mandatory to cover your head. It also keeps you safe from the sun and prying eyes of men.

Never reveal to people around you that you are lost and do not identify where you have to go to. If possible avoid travelling or venturing out on lonely streets after dark, especially on foot.

If you find a man staring at you, do not try to stare back or show any interest. I know it sounds strange but the best way out is to avert their gaze and get immersed in a book or look outside the window if you are on a train or coach. Any kind of response will only further encourage the pervert. But be alert.

Remember, Indian women do not often drink alcohol in public or with strangers. If someone offers you a drink, then their intentions may not be good. Also they may consider you to be of loose morals if you accept their offer thus encouraging their advances.

Keep your mobile fully recharged and have a speed dial help ready to use in case of emergency. Do not venture into areas where your mobile signal is lost. Don't hesitate to ask for help even if you are just sensing some danger. Better be safe than sorry.

Learn about the local culture of the area you are visiting and if possible, learn some basic language of the people.

Smart female tourists from countries all around the world have toured India and enjoyed its mystic and exotic beauty by following these very safety tips. The best way is to know the place well and adapt yourself to it.

Chapter 8: Avoiding culture shock in India

If you are travelling to India from the American continent or Europe, then you are in for a culture shock in India. Here are some of the things that you might expect in India and going through them will prevent you from getting a culture shock.

Shock at the airport

If you're going to India in the summer, then you will be surprised at the heat. If you are flying to Delhi then the temperatures can get very high even close to 50 degree centigrade. You will feel as if you are stepping into a sauna or an oven as soon you step out of the air-conditioned environment of the airport. I suggest you keep a handkerchief handy to wipe out the sweat.

Noise in India

We in India don't seem to mind noise. I remember studying for my exams while my neighbour was getting married who had Hindi music coming out of loudspeakers at full volume. You might awaken in the morning by the Muslim Azan (prayers) from the nearby mosque or Hindu bhazans being broadcasted from the temples.

Chaotic Indian roads

When you are on the roads, you cannot help noticing that Indian roads are chaotic. Horns are used extensively. It's nothing to do with rudeness, it's a method used to let other drivers that you are there. Unlike, Europe and USA, horns are used rarely or in extreme situations, horns in India is used every few minutes. Some drivers even have one hand on the steering wheel and the other on the horn. In addition, don't mind the unpleasant odour while riding a card from exposed rubbish on the side of the road.

The cows of India

In India, we like our cows but we don't eat them. Hindus revere the cows. There are multiple reasons for this. One of the reasons is that Krishna herded the cows and hence if the Lord liked cows, so do we. Secondly, once a baby leaves their mother's milk, they are given cow's milk and hence the cow is considered as a mother. You don't want to eat your mother do you? You will find many cows wandering around the roads as if they own the roads. Commuters and drivers don't seem to mind. However, I do not think there is any truth in the rumour that says that if you accidently hit a cow, you'll be imprisoned. You'll find other animals on the roads depending on where you're going from elephants to monkeys.

Urination on the side of the road

You'll find that this is allowed at some places. You will find men urinating on the side of road. Things are changing rapidly in India, public urinals are being built and awareness is being created. In larger cities, you will not find this as much as in smaller towns and villages.

Dirty public toilets

The public squat toilets in India are shockingly filthy. Men might be able to get away with it but women will probably have to wait till they get to a restaurant. However, there is a way round it. You might wish to take some of the female urination devices for your travels to India. Please read the section on how to use Indian toilets.

Indians live in communities such as large and joint families. This means that there is little thing called privacy. For instance, burping in public is considered rude in many countries, however many Indians consider burping as a necessity so don't be shocked to see Indians burp after they've had their meals. However, there is has been a shift in behaviour; many Indians are now beginning to realise that it's not a nice thing to do. Another interesting point, if you see two boys or men holding hands, that does not mean they're gay; they're just friends.

Poverty in India

In one minute, you will see sprawling sky scrapers and then the next minute, you will see beggars. You will be surprised to see the level of disparity between the people of India. You will soon realise that India is made of the destitute, the poor, middle class and the rich.

Religious practices

Unlike visiting churches or cathedrals, expect to take your shoes off if you're visiting temples, gurdwaras or mosques in India. We Indians consider the shoes as dirty and we take them off when entering houses of worship. Also cover your head with a scarf (not a cap) or the dupatta if you are wearing the Indian salwar kameez.

Haggling in India

You can haggle in India for prices depending where you're shopping. Unless you are shopping at outlets and multinational brands, you can bargain for prices in most Indian shops. The trick to this is to watch what others are paying. Give the vendor a price and work from there. Just walk away, if you're not happy with the price. You can also haggle for taxi, auto (three wheeler) and rickshaw fares.

I definitely recommend visiting India. It might be a culture shock for some but there is no place like India where you will see such bright colours, amazing people, history, culture and amazing food. You just need to open you heart a little and you'll have a trip of a lifetime.

Chapter 9: Travelling alone in trains

Travelling by train is one of the cheapest, most comfortable and the easiest way to explore the country. Indian railways, the fourth largest railway network in the world runs through all the states of India and allow the passenger to travel either in simple cheap means or the classic air-conditioned coaches which are excellent for long journeys. As the train runs through remote areas, villages, towns and jungles of India; you will be treated to a close look at the country and its diversity. Travelling by train is not just transportation but a great experience to relish and understand India. In fact, I can tell you that your tour of India will be incomplete without experiencing the bustling crowd at the railway station, seeing the hawkers selling food, listening to beggars singing soulful songs and looking at the sights of India fly past to the tune of the Indian Railways.

Indian trains have both good and bad reputation amongst the tourists, depending on the type of experience they have come across. The major complaint is about cleanliness as the compartments especially the general compartments are often dusty, has bad smells with stains of paan (betel leaf) in various corners of the trains. However, you don't have to face such problems in the luxury compartments though.

The second concern is about safety of travelling by trains. We often hear about people being assaulted, spiked and robbed or women being raped in the trains. This raises the question, 'is train travel safe for single women touring India?' The truth is that Indian trains are safe to travel provided that certain precautions are taken as suggested below.

Tourists do not have to worry about the crowded compartments where there are lots of people. It may seem as if it is going to burst with people. You often see people hanging out of doors or even sitting on the roof of the trains. These are usually the local trains which people use to travel to work, colleges or commuting short distances. The long distance trains are less crowded, more hygienic and also very comfortable.

Tourists have 8 different classes to choose from. For a solo female tourist, the two tier (air conditioned) A/C coaches are the best as far as comfort is concerned. It has decent bedding to sleep at night and there are curtains for privacy.

The A/C coaches allows you to book reservations, which means your seat is booked in advance; therefore you do not have to worry about the crowd. No one will take your seat. The A/C will provide relief from the heat, which can be threatening most of the time and is quite unbearable during the summer months. It is also safer, as you will always find an Indian family in this class who will be friendly and helpful. The air conditioned first class is a bit expensive, but the comfort makes up for the extra cost. It is often taken by business class people who are travelling alone.

Thefts and robberies are not common in Indian trains, but there are reports of it happening. As the tourists will be carrying their passports, credit cards and other important things with them, it is better to be safe than sorry. As a security against theft, you can always buy a cycle lock to secure you luggage, so that it will not be stolen when you are asleep. The Indian Railways keeping this in mind has provided hoops under the seats to which baggage can be secured. Also keep you baggage locked. Keep mobile phones and money with you at all times.

Being a foreigner, you will be targeted by scammers who will try to sell you things such as the souvenir items, or attempt to get you to book a guide, or tempt to take you to a hotel or sell you further tickets for sightseeing etc. Just don't give in to the scammers.

Never accept food or drinks from anyone, not even a friendly looking family. Drugging a lone woman is one of the most dangerous crimes that can happen especially on long distance trains. You can be robbed or worse it can end up in rape. Be cautious and be alert about the food you take.

Do not get too close to any men who will try to befriend you and get details about where you going etc. Many women have fallen prey to sweet talking Indian men and have ended up in tough situations.

Do not wear clothes that will expose too much of skin especially when you are asleep on the train. Basically when sleeping on trains cover yourself nicely. Last thing you want is you being photographed or stared at. Don't allow your legs to get uncovered and if you can, wear your day clothes. Also sleep lightly and keep an eye on your luggage. Keep your money, passport and tickets in a 'travel pouch' and hide it and carry them around at all times for example if you had to go to the toilet, take it with you. A zipped travel pouch that you can discretely fit securely around your waist is a good idea.

Some men are known to get some kind of sadistic pleasure in staring at women and making them uncomfortable. Just keep yourself well covered and ignore those stares as though you are not bothered.

When you go to the railway station, you might find the place confusing. There will be huge crowds with porters, vendors and travellers all at one place. Make sure that you arrive early and if you had to hire a porter, get an official one. You will know as they will have badges on them. They will also assist you find your seat.

All in all, travelling by train in India is safe but make sure you travel by A/C class and avoid non-A/C travelling. Finally carry yourself with confidence. Do not ask for details or instructions from fellow passengers unless you really have to. Better do all the research online and know all the information before hand. A nervous first time tourist is the target scammers will be looking for. Don't be one. Follow your heart and use common sense to do the right things and have a wonderful journey through incredible India.

Chapter 10: Groping in India and how to avoid it

Groping is harassing a person sexually by touching them inappropriately on parts of their body where they do not want to be touched and without their permission. In India, the law is very lenient on gropers. No wonder, this is a country where only 26% of rapists are convicted.

Taking advantage of this opportunity, gropers have become a menace on public transports and crowded places. The gropers often rub themselves against women, grab their legs, thighs, caress their buttocks or brush against their breasts very rudely and sexually. Tourists should be careful of being groped by Indian men in crowded places.

If you ask any woman in India about this menace they will have at least 3-4 incidences of such violation to tell you. Gropers are not just juvenile or the youth, but most of them are middle aged or old men. These people grab young girls, foreign tourists or anyone who looks unlikely to create problem for them. The uniform clad school going girls often have to face the menace where gropers slide hands up their thighs or touch their legs which is easily accessible through the uniform skirts. These innocent girls are ashamed to complain and often silently suffer the groping. Unfortunately, silence only encourages the gropers and they may target more women to this heinous crime.

Sadly, there are no strict laws which will punish the gropers therefore women in particular do not make a hue and cry about it. In addition, in highly crowded places it is very difficult to pin point the hand that is touching you.

Here are some tips that may help you to avoid groping:

First thing is, know that it is not your fault that you were groped. Do not feel ashamed to shout and call for help. If possible push and shout at the person. Being at a crowded place you can get help from fellow passengers. No person has any right to touch your body and play with it.

If you do not want to create a scene, poke the offender with whatever you can lay your hands on. Pinch, scratch or step on their toes if you can identify them. If you have an object with you, poke the exact part of the body that is touching you in self defence.

You have freedom to wear whatever makes you comfortable, but when you are getting in crowded buses, trains or markets, wear something that will not allow anyone to slide their hands into. This is exactly why I insist on wearing something that will not expose the skin too much.

Do not sit on the aisle seat which makes your breasts easy target to the hands of men who are passing by. If you do have to sit there, then put a guard in front of you so that your breasts are covered.

Most often the gropers are like professionals who can identify and prey on victims and attack those who are most vulnerable. They take advantage of the uncertainty, fear, surprise, shock, shame and confusion that strikes a person when they find they are being touched inappropriately. Look stern and confident which can deter a groper.

As for the government, they can introduce stricter laws to punish gropers when they are caught, especially for repeat offenders. Groping is an offence which violates the privacy of the women. Encouraged by getting away with it, these men may someday take one step ahead and turn into rapists. Therefore it would help a lot to nip the menace in the bud with imprisonment and fine for the men who are caught groping.

The separate buses and train compartments for women is quite a good initiative, but steps should be taken to make women feel safe in general places too.

There should be posters and signs warning innocent tourists of the ways of the gropers and how to react to them. Often they depend on the silence of the victim who is too stunned to react. Creating awareness will prevent the victims to suffer in silence. It is also important to train the general public to react strongly to this offence.

All in all, my advice is not use public transport such as the Delhi buses or local Mumbai trains and if you can, uses taxis and auto-rickshaws for getting around.

Chapter 11: What should female tourists wear in India

Women all over the world are fighting for their rights to live and dress as they want. Unfortunately, India is not yet a country to claim those rights to dress as you wish. Indians are still very conservative and traditional people especially those living in rural India - therefore wearing short skirts, tight tops or body revealing clothes is going to attract attention. This does not mean that women or girls in India do not wear revealing outfits - they do, it's just not as common in most parts of India other than metropolitan cities and some places such as Goa.

A tourist clad in body revealing clothes may get stared at, get whistled at and could even be groped by pervert men. Even Indian women give nasty stares when they see other women in scanty dress. So the best bet is to wear something that is acceptable in India. It is not much of a deal if you have to respect the local custom and dress accordingly for a few days while in India. As the old saying goes, 'When in Rome, do as the Romans do'.

As a female tourist travelling to India, you need not carry too many clothes in the first place. Basically what I am saying is that you don't have to carry a heavy baggage. You can buy and try on Indian dresses in India which are not very expensive and getting them washed is very cheap in India too. Even Western clothes are available in India and they are not very expensive either.

A female tourist may want to know which body part should be covered in India so that she may make changes to her style? To be on safer side, it is best to wear something that covers the shoulders, does not show cleavage and flows down at least up to the knees. Covering the head with a scarf is a good idea especially if you have blonde hair but not that important. A shawl or veil thrown around the shoulders is always a good bet. Metro cities have more open minded citizens; therefore you can go for shorts or tight tops if you feel like.

For women who love to try Indian dresses, there are wonderful kurtas (or kurtis) that go well with either Indian salwars or jeans. Created keeping Indian conditions in mind, they make you feel very comfortable. Also they can be bought in almost every color known in the spectrum. You can always carry them back to your country and wear them around especially when the weather gets hot. Make sure that these kurtis are covering your bottom.

Salwar Kameez is another popular Indian dress which comes in westernised styles. It has a knee length tunic worn with flared pants making it a very comfortable dress to be worn in Indian climates. Most salwar kameez is usually accompanied with a matching "dupatta", a kind of scarf that is used to cover the contours of the breast. The dupatta can be used to cover the head in the heat or when visiting religious places which requires covering of your hair.

Also there are knee-length and ankle-length skirts which may cost a lot in other countries but can be found at throw away prices in India at open bazaars and stalls. A top combined with ankle length skirt with a veil thrown over your shoulder will give you a classic traditional look.

Saris (sarees) are the special trademark of Indian women, and you should wear it at least once to feel the amazing fabric and the experience but never try this attire on your own. You will need the help of an Indian woman who is expert in wearing saris to try this on. If not, it may come apart leading to a tangled mess from which it would be difficult to get away. Wear the traditional "bindi" on the forehead, glass bangles and flowers in the hair for a photo session looking like an Indian. If you are attending a wedding the saris is a good idea.

For those who are not comfortable with Indian dresses; cotton shirts or T-shirts with jeans can blend in well, as more and more Indian women are opting for this fashion. It also protects you from the sun and heat. India is known for its mosquito population too so being fully covered protects you from the nasty bites.

Indian roads can be hard on your feet, so instead of going for fashionable footwear, you can wear comfortable shoes that will protect your feet from getting dirty. Some Indian roads can be messy especially during rainy season so come well prepared for it. If you are visiting homes or sacred places then go for cheap slip-ons, because you may have to take off your footwear before entering religious places such as durgahs, temples and even Indian homes. It is not very common for the footwear to get stolen in busy places.

Wear sunglasses as the Indian sun can glare you blind especially if you are coming from a cold country. It also prevents unwanted strangers making eye contact with you.

As for other accessories, the only care you have to take is to make sure that you do not carry a purse around in your hand which can be easily stolen or snatched. If you really wanted to carry a purse type of bag then you should carry something that you can strap around the shoulders. Rest of the other items will blend in India very easily.

Remember, shorts or miniskirts are still worn in the metros so it's not that Indian women don't wear them, it's all about trying to fit and preventing unwanted attention particularly if you are going to India on your own. You can buy some of these Indian clothes on Amazon and EBay if you want to buy them beforehand. If you are uncomfortable with wearing Indian clothes then you should just wear jeans or leggings with tops that cover the bottom.

Chapter 12: Travel safety items to take to India

If you are travelling to India, then I cannot stress hard enough about being safe. In recent months, a lot of negative news has been emerging from the media. Travelling can be a risky business anywhere let alone India. For instance, you can easily get shot dead in South Africa or Brazil, or get mugged in New York or groped in Manhattan. Jamaica being an extremely popular destination for beech holidays has a reputation for crime and murder while Mexico is perhaps one of the most dangerous cities in the world. If you thought Israel was safe, I found army bunkers at every mile where 16 year old recruits carried assault rifles; the threat of terrorist attacks over there was real. If you thought Russia was safe - it tops the 10 countries where kidnapping is high.

Most travellers in most part of the world do not face any issues but just one or two negative news is enough to put you off. India is still comparably safe and most travellers have the best times of their lives.

Here are some travel safety items you can carry with you to India:

If you are travelling in a foreign country, it's quite natural to feel vulnerable. These personal security items can provide some peace of mind and protection while travelling especially alone.

Internal door lock – If you think that you're the only one with the key to the room then you are mistaken. Any of the hotel staff can come in the room. Did you hear about the British women staying in a hotel in Agra (city where the Taj Majal is) – she had to jump out of the window because the hotel owner was trying to force himself in her room at 4 in the morning. This security item will allow you to lock yourself in and prevent unwanted intruders from coming in.

Door wedge or stopper - This simple device can be found in almost every single home in the world. If used in the reverse order, did you know that it has the power to stop someone from coming in! When you go to sleep, just nudge it under the door and prevent someone sneaking into the room while you are sleeping. You can also get something more advanced such as the alarmed "Super Door Stop Alarm" that activates when the door is forced open.

Personal alarm or whistle - A personal alarm also known as a rape alarm has a powerful sound that can deter potential attackers. Some of these alarms can emit very loud sounds emitting 130db which can be heard over half a mile away.

Flash light - A flash light can be a handy item to carry around and most travel experts recommend carrying one. Choose one that is small lightweight and durable, has good LED lit illumination, good beam focus and is water-resistant and one that does not consume batteries fast.

Travel smoke detector – Almost every home in the western world would have a smoke alarm. Unfortunately Indian homes or hotels do not have the same standards. Why not carry a mini or travel smoke alarm with you. Basically a smoke detector will alert you if there was a fire in your hotel.

Fake wedding ring – Although this will not deter criminals' hell bent on harming you but it might deter those trying to make a move to get you in bed. In India, some women wear fake "mangal sutras and wear vermillion" (symbols of marriage in India) on their foreheads to indicate that they are married. Usually married women do not attract as much attention compared to their unmarried counterparts.

First aid kit - Although doctors are available in every nook and corner of India, you must have travel insurance sorted out.

Also carrying a basic personal first aid kit with you can be a good idea.

Chapter 13: Don't forget these to India

When you plan of visiting an exotic country like India, most people usually think of packing a few things to wear and a camera to capture the amazing journey.

Unfortunately, this would lead to a lot of problems especially for those who are visiting for the first time. The time in India should be spent enjoying the place and not looking for essentials to buy. Therefore, check everything out beforehand and make a list of things you may need during your tour specially things that may not be available in India. At times even the tiniest of things like the electrical adapter to change the voltage of the electronics such as of the humble hairdryer can take half of your day. Worse still, you may never find it. Instead of running around looking for things, it is wise to bring them along with you, so that your trip could be enjoyed without any frustration.

Here is a list of essentials you should not forget to bring to India:

Get yourself few guide books, maps and itineraries of the places you plan to visit. Knowing where you are going and walking confidently in the place, will keep you safe. Also learn about currency rates, travel timings etc which will prevent people from duping you. Try to get accustomed to the local language with a dictionary. I have already included some Hindi words and phrases that you will find useful.

Make few Xerox (photo) copies of visa, passport and other important documents and distribute it among your luggage to be on safer side.

Travel pouches are very handy specially the ones that can be hidden discretely under the belt. Pickpockets are a menace and you should have your money and travel documents hidden away. You could also have some special leg pouches, or 'bra pouches for travel' to keep your money safe under your clothing.

Pack clothes keeping in mind the Indian traditions and culture. Make sure you pack your favorite scarf as it comes in handy in many ways if you plan to visit religious places.

Be prepared for power cuts which can throw you into darkness without any warning, especially in rural India. You can always carry a pen torch or something similar which you can use in times of such crisis. Nowadays, some mobile phones come with a torch which can be used temporarily. You can also a bring wind up flashlight radio.

Cameras are trademark of tourists; therefore there is no need to mention it in the list. What you may forget to pack is an extra pack of batteries or converter for your camera if it is rechargeable one. In rural India it will be very tough to find the exact matching batteries or converters.

Pack your over the counter medicines, face creams, sun screen, shampoo, and other things for regular use. Do not forget to include anti-diarrhea medicine and mosquito repellent cream in your list. Most of the time, you will not be able to find the exact thing you are used to in a new country. You don't want to end up with an allergy by using products that do not suite you. There is lot of fake brands in India, which could create problems to the skin or cause hair damage.

You could always bring your own tampons; as they are not very common in India.

If you wear glasses or contact lenses, bring an extra pair. Also pack in your sunglasses because chances are that you will need it.

If you are worried about thefts, than it is a good idea bringing your own locks. Thieves get confused with unknown models and may consider it not worth the trouble to open it. If you are worried about security of your room, then you can buy various door stoppers, burglar alarms and other such accessories which may warn you about intruders (see chapter 'Travel safety items to take to India' for details).

Dry gear bags are very useful if you are planning on visiting beaches or during rainy seasons.

Toilet rolls will come in handy. Indians don't use toilet rolls and hence you might wish to bring some of these to India. Although you can buy them but they are not readily available especially in smaller towns and rural areas of India. At some stage of your trip to India, you will have to use the Indian squat toilet so don't forget to read the section on how to use it.

Travelling in trains or buses during long journey may be noisy for a foreigner. Indians love to honk the horns and talk out loud during travel. Bring few ear-plugs or iPods which can save you from unwanted noise.

Chapter 14: Safety tips for Indian hotels

A hotel is a place where you must feel safe but safety cannot be guaranteed and these days - you just cannot be too sure and women travelling alone have to be extra careful. It's not being paranoid but being practical.

Here are some hotel safety tips to prevent hotel crime. Some may sound overdramatic but it's still worth a mention.

Always stay in a hotel that is on the main road.

Try to get a room near the stairs or the lift just in case you want to run away. Also if you can, try not to get a room on higher floors. Remember the woman from Britain in Agra who jumped out of the hotel. If she had been on one extra floor, it is definite she could have injured herself. But obviously if you are staying in a well known hotel then chances are that you will be safe.

Try not to eat particularly the dinner at the hotel or at least make sure that there are lots of guests staying at the hotel. You never know what could be in the food. Some hotel owner might try to put some drugs or sleeping tablets in the food and try to take advantage of you when you are sleeping. If you have your dinner elsewhere, chances are that they do not know where you are staying. You will have to make a judgment call there and then.

Keep jewellery out of site. Make sure that your jewellery is hidden away. Try not to wear gold rings, necklaces to India or at least keep them hidden away from sight from hotel staff.

Don't let anyone come in the room other than the hotel staff.

Always carry the hotel details, you can ask for a hotel business card.

If there is a telephone, make sure it's working. If not, enquire why it's out of order.

Don't let the hotel staff publicise your room number to prevent others knowing which room you are staying in.

Check the door if they lock. Make sure the window opens and take a peep outside. Also make sure they are closed before you go to sleep.

Make a mental picture of the inside of the hotel. Pay particular attention to the halls, the way the rooms are arranged, the stairs, the lifts, possible escape routes. Imagine, if you had to run – how and what would you do?

Keep your shoes near the bed just in case you need to make a run for your life. I know it sounds dramatic but you never know.

Keep your keys under the pillow so that you have access to it all the time. Do not leave it hanging on the door.

Don't open the door to anyone who you are unsure off.

Make sure you have your passport and money is safe when you are sleeping.

Don't leave your valuables in the room while on excursion – take them with you.

Try to book your hotels under the name of Mrs. to let the hotel staffs know that you are married. Wear a cheap wedding ring to ward of male attention.

Do not display valuables in the open such as iPad, laptops or other expensive gadgets. When you are using room service make sure that they are hidden away before you open the room. Basically don't let it out in full view. Last thing you want is to let a room boy or any hotel staff feeling tempted to commit a crime.

You could take photos of the hotel from outside and inside for evidence if required in case of a crime.

Avoid dangerous situations in general.

Remember if someone late at night knocks on the door – shout at them and ask them what they want. Tell them do go away at the top of your voice. Do not open the door no matter what. No one should be knocking on the door late at night specially men. In the morning, tell the manager and ask them why someone was knocking so late at night and you intend to tell the police if this happens again. If you find the hotel to be unsafe - LEAVE and find another hotel on the main road.

Chapter 15: How to defend yourself in dangerous situations

Unfortunately there are plenty of unsavoury characters out there, many of whom have strange tendencies to harm other people. Many experts suggest that women follow some sort of self defence class, and I suggest you do that too! However, please do read the tips that follow. Whilst it is unlikely that you will be attacked, if you consider these tips and you do get into trouble then you will know what to do.

Never underestimate the power of your elbow. This is one of the 'hardest' parts of your body. If you have a chance, elbow your attacker. It will knock them back a little, which may provide you time to run away or summon help.

If you are being mugged and somebody asks for your phone or wallet, then give it to them. Don't argue about it, this is just going to lead to you being hurt. Don't hand it straight into their hands though, instead throw it away from yourself. The person will run to grab your wallet or phone, which is going to give you time to escape. After they have your wallet, it is unlikely that they will care about you anyway unless they want something else.

Don't stay still if you have been attacked by a person with a gun. Run away! I know it may seem scary, but it is highly unlikely that the person will hit you with the weapon as you run, especially if you run in a 'zig zag' like pattern! Run far enough and eventually you will end up in a place where the person will stop firing, they may even run out of ammunition before you get there.

Kick the groin! If there is one way to take a man out, it is kicking a man here. Get a good hit in and they will be out for minutes, which of course are going to give you the perfect amount of time to get out of there. For some reason, many women are reluctant to hit this area, but trust me it is one of the only ways in which you are going to be able to overpower your attacker.

If you feel as though somebody is following you, don't approach them. Instead, find a safe location full of people that you can go into. If you still feel as though you are being followed then mention it to somebody, they will be able to deal with the problem for you!

Stairs are an absolutely horrendous location as you really don't know what is lurking there in the dead of night. Elevators have CCTV, which means that very few people will risk attacking somebody else. But mind you, many if not all elevators in India may not have these CCTVs. So again you will have to make judgment call and decide for yourself there and then. Basically, be careful if you are on a flight of stairs.

When you get into your vehicle if you have hired one, lock the doors straight away especially late at night. This is different to Western countries where you don't lock the car from inside just in case there is an accident but in India it's different. It's more about preventing other people harming you.

Use common sense! Perhaps one of the best tips I can offer you. This means not going to dark, empty locations by yourself, and of course, not heading outside alone at night unless you absolutely need to do so!

As you can see, many of these tips were focused on escaping, which I feel is the way it should be. After all, you don't want to stick around too long, you will be overpowered if you are not careful, and this of course going to put you in a lot of danger.

Chapter 16: Practical Hindi for your travels in India

The basics

Hello = Namaste or Pranaam

Morning = subhah

Night = raat

Left = baiye

Right (direction) = daiye

Yes = haa

No = nahi

Good = accha

Today = aaj

Tomorrow = kal

Temple = mandir

Local = desi

Time = samay

Okay/good/whatever = thik hai

Stop= ruko

Please = kripya

Thank you = dhanyevad or shukriya

Sorry or Excuse me = maaf kijiye

Food and drink

Tea = chai

Sugar = cheeni

Water = pani

Chapattis = roti

Rice = chawal or bhaat

Food = khaana

Breakfast = naasta

Greetings

What's your name = app ka kya naam hai

My name is Shalu = mera naam Shalu hai

How are you = aap kaisi hai

I am fine = mai thik hu

We'll meet again = phir milenge

I am going = mai jaa raha hu (male); mai jaa rahi hu (female)

I am from America = mei America se hu

Nice to meet you = aap se milke khusi hui

How's your family= aap ka parivar kaise hai?

Words/phrases that you might use when shopping in India

Any discount = daam kum kijiye

How much or what is the cost = kitnay ka hai

This is expensive = yeh bahut mehanga hai

Bill please - bill de dijiye

What happened = kya hua

I want a ticket = mujhe ek ticket chahiye

How much is this = ye kitne ka hai

Out and about

Let's go = chalo

Go away = chale jayo

Get lost = chal bhaag (just in case if you want to use it)

Please take me to my hotel = kripya mujhe mera hotel le chaliye

I need a taxi = mujhe ek taxi chahiye

I don't know = mujhe nahi malum

Who are you = aap kaun hai

I understand = samagh gaye

Where is the toilet = toilet kidhar hai

Leave me alone = mujhe akela chhor do

I am coming = mai aa raha hu (male); mai aa rahi ho (female)

What are you thinking = aap kya sooch rahe hai

How to get to the station = station ka rasta bataiye

0 = shunya

1 = ek

2 = do

3 = teen

4 = char

5 = panch

6 = cchhai

7 = saath

8 = aath

9 = nau

10 = dus

Help words in Hindi

Madad – Help

Mujhe madaad chahiye - I need help

Kya aap meri madad kar saktay hai? – can you help me?

Bachao – Save (<u>Bachao Bachao</u> to be used in distress meaning "save me")

Mujhe bachaoo – help me

Balaatkar - Rape

Mera balatkar hua hai – I have been raped

Ajnabi – Stranger

Aspatal – Hospital

Mujhe aspatal le chaliye – take me to the hospital

I'm lost - Mai kho gaya hu (male), Mai khi gayi hui (female)

I need a doctor - Mujhe ek doctor chaiye

Police station kidhar hai? - Where is the police station?

I want water - Mujhe paani chahiye

Bhago - Lets run

Hum log kaha hai – where are we?

I didn't understand – Mujhe samajh nahi aaya

Can you speak slowly? – Kya aap dheera deera bol sakte hai

I am lost – Mai khogayi hu (female), mai kho gayi hu (Mai kho gaya hu)

Go away – Chale jayo

I can't speak Hindi – Mujhe Hindi nahi aati

Where is the telephone booth? – Telephone booth kaha hai?

Atankvaadi – Terrorists

Others

I want a ticket - Mujhe ticket chahiye

Where is the toilet - Bathroom kaha hai

I am from USA - Main USA se hoon

How much is this? - Ye kitne ka hai

How are you? - Aap kaise hain?

I don't speak Hindi - Mujhe hindi nahi aati hai

Do you speak English? - Kya app English bolte hai

How old are you? - Aap ki umar kya hai

I have to go - Mujhe jaana hai

One moment - Ek minute

Hurry up – Jaldi karo

What time is it? - Time kya hua

Toilet – Latrine

You can listen to the pronunciation to some of these words and phrases on my blog (http://www.shalusharma.com/hindi-phrases).

Chapter 17: Travelling with kids in India

More and more women are now living alone with kids and every now and then they need to travel with children.

Tourists who plan to visit India have to take certain precautions regarding their paperwork, advance booking, vaccines and also collecting information about the place they are visiting. When they have young children accompanying them, these precautions will need some extra additions keeping the safety of their children in mind. Touring India with children is not like visiting just any other country- this is India. It is advisable to be prepared and know in advance what you are getting into with your children.

In order to prevent culture shock to the children, show them pictures and videos about India before they come to India. Most of these videos can be seen on YouTube. Children coming to India from developed nations may find it difficult to accept the level of poverty. The language, noise, and body language of the people may confuse the children. It is possible that they may feel threatened and scared. Therefore, it is better to keep them well informed about what to expect.

The excitement of the new environment, food, places and the tour itself can fill the children with enthusiasm. This will lead them to try out new things and hence cause them to drop their guard. Special care should be taken to see that the children do not go overboard in trying all the new food which could be tough on their tummies. It is also important to keep an eye on the children all the time as new unfamiliar place could prove dangerous.

The most important part of the travel plan is the immunisation of children as they are more vulnerable to infections and illness than adults. Apart from their regular immunisation program, they may require some extra immunisation and vaccinations keeping in mind the prevalent diseases of the travel destination. It is wise to get them vaccinated before embarking on the trip. The last thing you would want on your tour is sick and fussy children.

Check out the list of routine vaccines to see if they interfere with your touring dates

Measles, mumps, rubella (MMR)

Meningitis C

4-in-1 pre-school booster flu shot

5-in-1 vaccine

BCG (tuberculosis) vaccination

Make sure you have not missed on the important travel vaccines

Hepatitis A vaccination

Hepatitis B vaccination

Polio vaccination

Malaria

Typhoid vaccination

Rabies vaccination

Tetanus vaccination

Explain to the children about the dangers involved in drinking unhygienic water, eating food from road side restaurants and stalls and to check for seals before consuming any packaged food. Even if they have the immunisations, they are still prone to infection. Try to eat at hotels that have good reputation for serving hygienic food. If the children do not like to try new food, then there is always KFC, McDonald's, Subway and other global eateries available in most places in India. Keep the children well hydrated as they can easily get dehydrated in the hot Indian climatic condition especially during the summer. Make sure you and the children wash your hands before eating. I carry my own soap with me and try not to use the soap at public places. Liquid soap from the dispensers is fine.

Children can get hungry all of a sudden even after a full meal, especially when they are travelling. So carry packaged food items and fresh fruits with you at all times. Always keep bottled water at all times.

No amount of tissues and wipes are ever going to be enough for children in a country like India. Make sure that you have sufficient supplies of toiletries that will last for a day or two at least. Carry a small towel at all times if have to.

Some children are prone to falls, cuts and bruises. Keep a first aid kit stacked away in your backpack for any emergency. See that you have enough basic medications, anti-septic creams, band-aids and anti-pyretic syrup in the first aid box.

The delicate skin of children can get easily burnt in the harsh Indian sun. Carry sun screens, hats and glasses to avoid sun burn.

The common western toilets may not be available everywhere in India. It is important to tell the children about the squat toilets. Most of the children are scared of falling down when they see it for the first time. I have written about using the Indian squat toilet on my blog and included in the book.
http://www.shalusharma.com/how-to-use-the-indian-squat-toilet

Protect them against mosquitoes and other insect bites. Buy mosquito nets or creams that repel mosquitoes and apply it on the skin at night.

Children can adjust their body clocks to the new timing and surrounding much more easily than the adults so be prepared to be nagged out of bed.

Finally be prepared to hear things like "I am bored" or "I don't want to be here". So keep books, games or something to entertain them. The biggest complaint from them will be about the heat so make sure you keep them hydrated.

Chapter 18: Travel scams in India

Even an experienced and well informed tourist may get scammed at one time or other while touring India. Most of the first time travellers to India become easy victims to scammers as they are unaware of the ways and methods by which the scammers function. Some of them may approach the jetlagged and confused tourist as a well wisher before showing their true colors and cheating them. Beware of people who try to give you unsolicited, unasked or unrelated advice. Never give clues that you are visiting India for the first time, as that will only encourage the scammers to go ahead with their vicious schemes.

The most common form of scam begins at the airport itself when the tourist hires a taxi. Most of the tourists have reservation at hotels and often hire taxis to take them there. At first, the taxi driver says they know the place very well, but then they start taking the tourist to different places pretending that they do not understand what the tourist is saying. Often they stop to ask directions in local languages which could be about some other place. The tourist will see and understand the wave of hand showing directions. As the taxi moves round and round the town while the bill keeps mounting up. The taxi driver may start blaming the tourist for misguiding him by not giving proper address. Finally when they arrive on their destination, the driver will demand extra money for the trouble he has been put through. Some of the tourists have actually generously tipped the drivers believing that the driver could not follow their accent and hence went through all the trouble.

The best solution is to hire taxi with GPS or prepaid taxis available in all major cities of India. With advanced technology, any traveller can now know the route through maps on mobile applications. Doing some research and knowing about the area you are travelling will prevent scammers from taking advantage.

Unfortunately, prepaid taxis are not fool-proof and you still can be scammed.

Any auto-rickshaw or taxi driver, who promises lowest fare is sure to take you at least to 5-6 shops or emporiums on the way to your destination. The trick is the commission offered by the shop keeper to the drivers for bringing them customers. Often they are very persistent and may end up selling you things that you may later regret buying. Also you may waste a lot of time looking at things in the shops and be late to your destination. Be careful especially if you are going to the railway station or the airport as you might miss your transportation.

Another popular trick used by the taxi or auto rickshaw drivers is to tell the tourist that the hotel or place they have booked has been closed down or it is dangerous. They will come up with new addresses with lucrative offers which may tempt the tourist. Never believe such people, as they are trained scammers. Tell them that you have a friend or colleague waiting for you at the predetermined destination. If you do not arrive on time, they may panic and lodge a complaint with the police or something to that effect. Just make sure that the scammer understands that you are not going to budge from your decision.

The duty free allowance of the tourist has brought up the Gem Stone scam in India, especially in places like Agra and Jaipur as often people visit these places to buy gem stones. Either the person asks the tourists to take the gems with them under their duty free allowance to sell at some address for high profits, or they ask for some kind of financial assistance for exporting these gems. Most often the tourists end up losing the money or get stuck with gems for which they have paid much higher amount than their original price.

Some scammers pretend to be the employees on trains, tourist spots etc and try to collect fines, funds or upgrading fees from the tourists. The travellers who are new to the place may fail to recognise the difference in uniform. Do not pay fines or money to people who may be pretending like authority figures unless you are very sure of them. Check their ID and ask the locals if you have to.

People who offer help to show your destination and insist on helping you are more often the agents of a tourist agency. They will never take you to the actual destination but will often lead you the travel agency to collect their own commission. Genuine helpers never stand around waiting to help others but will do so when you ask them. Also they have no reason to insist on helping you. When was the last time you were looking around for people to help?

Some of these scammers are thick headed and no match for the smart tourist. You should be able to pick up some of the clues or hints that they are scam artists. Be on your guard and carry yourself with confidence to enjoy your visit to India.

Chapter 19: Diseases to beware of in India

Tourists planning on visiting India often spend their time looking for details on tourist spots, what to eat, things to do and where to go when visiting India. Unfortunately, what they forget to conduct research on is about the local diseases. The local people are often exposed to the virus and germs of these infectious agents giving their body immunity from these provincial diseases. The foreign tourists who are being exposed to these infectious germs will get infected and suffer from illness very easily. It is very important to find information on issues regarding health and safety when travelling to India.

India is a great place to visit due to its diversity not only in landscape, flora and fauna but also its rich culture, traditions and heritage. Unfortunately there are certain diseases a tourist has to be wary of when touring India.

Due to the rampant poverty and densely populated areas, many places have stagnant water which facilities the breeding of mosquitoes. Therefore malaria is a risk factor for tourists visiting India if they do not take proper precautions against mosquito bites. Find out information regarding endemic malarial data of the area you plan to visit. Search for the term "*India Malaria Map*" on Google and you will get a heat map of the places at risk. Basically in short, malaria is rampant throughout the country including cities of Mumbai and Delhi.

Take precautionary medicines at all costs. Since 1993 there have been 16 reported cases of death due to malarial infection among foreign tourists visiting India. Wearing insect repellent cream while going outdoors can easily protect a person from mosquito bites and malarial infection. Mosquito repellents are available everywhere in India as they not only help in keeping the mosquitoes at bay throughout the night but also give out pleasant fragrance that allows one to sleep peacefully.

It is common to see the sign 'Drinking Water' above various taps and filters strewn across bus-stands, railway stations and other public places in India. Many Indians do survive drinking this water, but unfortunately it can prove fatal to tourists leading to them being infected with waterborne diseases such as diarrhea, cholera and jaundice and the common 'Delhi belly'.

Though most of the tourists prefer bottled mineral water and avoid drinking unhygienic water, what they tend to forget is the same unhygienic water goes into the food or other beverages they may consume. Though the health department of India has taken strict measures to control and prevent outbreaks of waterborne diseases, the incidences are still on the rise. So you will have to be careful what you eat and where you eat. If the place looks dirty, it probably is – avoid it.

Open sewages, improper disposal of garbage and unhygienic sanitary system has led to cholera spreading quickly in many places in India, at times gaining epidemic proportions. Tourists need to take precautions against cholera even if it is not prevalent in the area they are visiting, as the disease has high fatality rate. It is highly beneficial if the tourist takes oral cholera vaccine before visiting a place that has risk of cholera. The vaccine provides immunity against infection for nearly 4-6 months.

Many of the stray dogs who roam the streets of India may carry the rabies virus which can spread to humans. In recent years, 3 British tourists have died after contracting rabies in India which led to WHO issuing travel warning to tourists visiting India. At present it is recommended that tourists be immunised against rabies infection before visiting the country. Once the symptoms appear, the disease is fatal even in intensive care. Hence pre-exposure immunisation is necessary for travellers especially for those who may come in contact with animals.

Tuberculosis is still claiming lives in India outbreaks are common in many places. The disease is spread through close contact with infected person or through unpasteurised milk. Tourists who visit India and stay in community housing need to take proper precautions regarding this contagious lung disease.

Typhoid is a waterborne disease often spread through human waste infecting the water; therefore tourists visiting rural areas are at high risk of being infected. Avoiding uncooked or partially cooked food and drinking only bottled or boiled water can ensure safety from typhoid. But it is always safe to take the typhoid vaccine. The oral vaccine will provide protection for a year whereas injections will keep a person safe for many years.

Although medical facilities have improved in the past few decades and at present available in every remote village of India, nevertheless it is safe to keep medicines for minor ailments and first aid ready with you as a precautionary measure. Planning a proper preventive inoculation through proper consultations with a doctor/nurse specialised in travel protection will ensure your safe travel.

Chapter 20: Terrorist attacks and abductions of tourists in India

Terrorism has been a looming problem in India. The insurgents and terrorists resort to hostage taking and kidnapping often of foreigners to put pressure on the government to bow down to their demands. At times, the country has been caught in very sticky situations often releasing hard core criminals and terrorists to release hostages. The terrorist attacks by Islamic hardcore terrorists have claimed 4,602 lives so far, injuring 10,388 people.

There have been terrorist attacks in India and also from Naxalite (Maoist insurgents who want to topple the government and establish communist rule) involving Indian and foreign citizens. Certain areas have been renowned for naxalite activities whereas Jammu and Kashmir is noted for terrorist groups alleged to be aided by neighboring Pakistan. They often target areas which are frequented by foreigners to gain international publicity.

The attack on Mumbai on the 26th of November 2008 left 166 people dead and 293 wounded also left 28 foreigners dead while injuring 27. The attack appeared to target not only Indians but also Americans, Britons, Australians and Jews in India. It also proves that threat of terror is always present in India and the terrorists can strike anywhere, anytime as it is nearly impossible to block all the loop holes present in the security system of the country.

60 people were killed in Jaipur, when a series of bombs went off in May 2008. The Bangalore serial blasts were less horrific with no heavy casualties though it did spread fear among the people to a great extent in July 2008. In the same month and year, twenty bombs exploded in the city of Ahmedabad in Gujarat, killing 50 people. Few months later in September 2008, 20 people lost their lives to five bombs planted by terrorists in different

places. The attack on the German Bakery in Pune in 2010 witnessed foreign casualties and it appears that they were the main targets when observed closely.

More recently, there were casualties in the terrorist attacks in Varanasi in December 2010, another attack on Mumbai once again in July and Delhi in September 2011. After a break of two years they surfaced once again in Hyderabad in February 2013.

On 13th March 2013, two terrorists dressed like cricket players entered the CRPF (India's central armed police forces) camp and attacked the CRPF men and locals with grenades and AK-47s killing 5 people in Srinagar.

The abductions came into lime light when two Swedish nationals, working as engineers in the Uri Hydel Project were kidnapped by a terrorist group from Baramulla on March 31, 1991. This was the first major incident that came into limelight in recent times. Fortunately, they were released after a great deal of negotiations.

In the following months on June 26th 1991, 8 tourists were abducted from the houseboat on Dal Lake. The abducted victims resisted the attack in which they killed two terrorists and escaped. However an Israeli national who was killed in the fight!

In 1994, an American tourist Stephen Paul was killed by terrorists near Srinagar.

The first such incident that turned into breaking news all over the world was the kidnapping of 6 foreign nationals – John Childs (USA), Dirk Hasert (Germany), Hans Christian Ostro (Norway) Keith Mangan (UK), Don Hutchings (USA) and Paul Wells (UK) - by a lesser known terrorist group who called themselves Al-Faran, in July 1995 from South Kashmir. They demanded release of the founder of a terrorist group known as Jaish-e-Mohammed, Maulana Masood Azar. Of the six victims, only John Childs was fortunate enough to escape from the clutches of the terrorists. The beheaded body of Ostro was found on 13th August. The fate of the other captives is still unknown. It is assumed that they were killed and buried somewhere in the region.

On 11th July 2000, a German tourist was kidnapped from Rangdum in Kargil area and killed the next day by terrorists. No one claimed to be responsibility.

The North-Eastern states of India have been subjected to lawlessness and violence due to the ULFA and Bodo Liberation Front militants who have abducted and killed many estate owners and businessmen in the last few years.

There was a series of low intensity bomb attacks on the famous Mahabodhi Temple complex in Bodh Gaya (Bihar) in July 2013 where foreign tourists from Buddhist countries frequently visit.

The risks of terrorist attacks are high in cities such as Mumbai, Delhi, Kolkata, Bangalore, Hyderabad and Chennai despite the security being stepped up. The rural areas have been spared of these demonic attacks so far. However, the fear of abductions and kidnappings in the remote areas is still there.

In March 2012, Italian tourists Paulo Bosusc and Claudio Colangelo were abducted while trekking in the resort of Daringibadi in Kandhamal area of Orissa (Odisha). There have been other incidences when foreign tourists were abducted and later released safely. To be on the safer side, the tourists should avoid areas which are supposed to be at high risk for terrorist attacks or abductions. These include Northeastern states (Assam, Arunachal Pradesh, Mizoram, Nagaland, Meghalaya, Tripura, and Manipur), Kashmir and active areas of Maoist extremist groups of southern Odisha.

They should not travel alone in dangerous zones. Giving chance for the terrorists to abduct them will not only put their lives in danger but also may result in release of dangerous terrorists who may end up taking more innocent lives in the future.

Chapter 21: How to report a crime to the police

Reporting a case to the police is very easy in India. Any information that needs to be reported to the police is done so, by lodging an FIR. This FIR can be lodged by the police, the witness or the victim.

FIR is the abbreviation for "First Information Report" which is a document written in black and white. Any cognisable offense is to be reported to the police in this way. This information is brought to notice by the police for the first time, thus coining of the term First Information Report (FIR). The First Information Report can be lodged either orally or in writing. They can also be reported telephonically. Lodging an FIR is the first step in bringing justice to a criminal action. The police then takes up to investigating the case after an FIR is registered. Anybody who knows what a cognisable offense is can report an FIR. Any police officer who gets firsthand knowledge about the offense can also register the FIR themselves. You can lodge the FIR if the crime is committed against you. You can lodge it if you are witness to the crime or know about a crime that has been committed.

The FIR is to be filed according to the procedures prearranged in section 154 of the Criminal Procedure Code (1973). Any information reported to the police orally needs to be written down by the police. The right to information gives every person a right to demand the police to read back the recorded information provided by them. Any information recorded by the police should be signed over by the information provider.

Cognisable offense is any offense which when reported to the olice may lead to an arrest by the police without warrant. The police may then formally start their investigation without having to take any further orders from the court. On the other hand, in the non-cognisable offense - police can't arrest anyone without a warrant. They need a warrant approved by the court to arrest somebody.

I just hope you do not have to go through this but if you did, here are the procedures you will need to know for reporting a crime (FIR) in India.

So what exactly do you need to lodge an FIR

You have to mention your name and current address

The date, time and place where the incident being reported happened

The information provided by you should be close to accurate

Descriptions and/or names if any of other persons caught up in the incident.

Do not provide any information that is misleading to the police or lodge a bogus complaint. The court has the right to prosecute you under Section 203 of the Indian Penal Code (1860). Do not overstate or twist any facts. You might land in trouble for making uncertain and vague statements. If you are not able to register an FIR, then you can bring your problems to notice by writing to the Superintendent of Police or any other officers of equivalent rank or higher. If the police are turning a blind eye, you can write to or submit your complaint to the National Human Rights Commission.

Don't forget to inform your embassy or your consulate about any incidences.

Chapter 22: How to deal with beggars

You want to spend your vacations at some exotic place. "Why not India?" you think. The country is old, it's big, it's diverse, it's not ruled by dictators, it possesses some unique customs and people speak English. (At least in big cities and the educated class.) You spend a few months saving for your dream vacation. Finally the day arrives. You land in your dream city. This is a magical place. Your hotel sends a cab, it takes you to the hotel. After taking a bath and some rest, you decide to take a walk in the bazaars. A kiosk catches your attention. You want to taste local food. You order something and expect it to be a great dish. You are about to take your first bite when you notice someone stretching an empty palm towards you. Before you can react, there are one, two, three, four... a whole sea of palms. Happy vacation!

You forget about eating and look at the person. He is dark skinned, very weak and usually a cripple. If she is a woman, you will notice her many children alongside. You wonder what to do? You don't want to give your food and wait for another half-an-hour before new order arrives. But you can't disappoint them. They are hopefully looking at you. Grudgingly you offer them food. To your surprise, they refuse!

At first you don't understand. However, soon you realise they are not here for food. They want money. You don't want to give them money. They may use it to buy drugs and what not. By this time, you are already surrounded by them. Shouting may make matters worse; this isn't your hometown or state or country. You want to get out of this mess as quickly as possible. You politely tell them you don't have change. They offer you change! You are stupefied. You can't tell if they are beggars or businesspeople. In desperation to rush out of it, you offer them a hundred-rupee note, tell them to divide among themselves and run as fast as your legs permit.

What tourists can do?

Beggars are found everywhere, even in rich countries. In India, situation is particularly bad. It's worse if you are a tourist. Start praying if you look different and don't speak the local language. You are bound to encounter them every time you set foot on the street. You are a kind person. You want to help. But you may not have the money to satisfy everyone, or you don't want to give money but still want to help.

If that's the case, here are a few handy tips:

Offer food: If a beggar accepts food, you have already helped. If they want money, they will refuse your food and go. You can give them a packet of biscuit if they are willing to take it. Genuine beggars will take it.

Don't stare them in the eye: Some beggars will refuse to leave and continue to nag. In that case, don't look them in the eye. Do what you are doing, if you are walking continue to walk; if you are eating keep on eating; pretend they don't exist.

Ask them to bring their chums and then pay them a small amount and tell them to divide among themselves. This way, you can ensure you will not have to deal with another beggar in that area.

Give them a small amount of money: If you really wanted to give them money, you can give them some change up to about 2 to 10 rupees. Remember many have been uplifted out of poverty but genuine beggars do exist. You will be able to distinugist between the real and fake ones. The fake ones will be full and appear able-bodied with no physical signs of handicap. While the genuine beggar will have a limb amputated and will look genuine. It is here that if wanted, you can hand them a 10-20 rupee note.

Don't give anything at all: Just walk away and do not do anything at all. Many Indians follow this rule. They simply refuse to hand any money to the beggars and if you wanted you could follow this rule.

Chapter 23: How to use Indian squat toilets

In most hotels around the country, you would find the flush type toilets or as they are often called the Western type toilets. So as long as you keep to such hotels, you needn't worry about the precarious scenario of having to use the 'Indian Style' or 'Squat Type Toilets'. But it is also true that there will be places in your itinerary where there would be no other option or from using cheaper hostels and hotels resulting in having to use the Indian styled toilet.

Often we have found the foreign visitors apprehensive and worried about using these toilets. But the fact of the matter is it isn't as hard as it seems and in many ways is more hygienic than the sit-down toilets. You will find the Indian toilets in most public places for example if you are travelling to the Taj Mahal and if you stop at some of the road side dhabas (places to eat) something like the motorway services, you will encounter them. You will find them in many trains too.

A squat toilet is a toilet used by squatting, rather than sitting. They consist essentially of a hole in the ground. Compared to the Western styled toilets, you have to sit down in a squat position. It's definitely not the most comfortable position for those who have not done it before but for Indian's it's a natural position. You might try this - if you have lifted weights before then try doing the half-squat and then the full squat. First try positioning in the half-squat position and then going down to the full-squat position. Try this technique several times.

There are two ways to use the toilet.

a) Slide you pants to the knees and sit down in the squat position. You have to remember to sit in such a way that you have your bum aiming at the hole so everything you dump goes straight down.

b) Alternately, take your pants off and hang it on a clip or the hook most usually found on the back of the door. Then crouch down and sit down in a squatting position. I prefer this method as you can be sure not to soil your clothes. Indian children are taught this method before they are competent to do it without taking their pants off.

After you finish defecating, use the shower spray connected to the toilet tank to clean the back side or you could carry your own toilet paper if not provided by the hotel. In many places you have won't have water sprays so you will have to use your own toilet paper or use the mug and bucket provided! So make sure that you have plenty of water before you sit down.

In order to wash your back side, pour water into your left hand from the mug and take it down to the backside and wash it. Repeat this as many times as it takes to clean your bum. I understand that you might not have tried this before so make sure when you have washed and you are completely satisfied, get up and wash your hands thoroughly.

After that, just flush or fill a mug or bucket with water and clean the toilet. Basically pour lots of water down to flush it.

I understand that it's not easy as it sounds and it may take some time to get used to but it isn't that bad after all considering that it is in fact hygienic. So be a good girl and do it at the hotel so you don't need a dump when you are out there.

For women who don't want to use these toilets for urinating, you can always carry female urinary devices (FUD) to use where you feel that using these toilets is not for you. There are several types of FUD such as Shewee, Go Girl, Whiz Freedom, P-Mate Female Disposable Urine Director, Lady Elegance and so on. You can read more about it on my blog here http://www.shalusharma.com/female-urination-devices-for-your-travels-to-india.

Chapter 24: Final words for solo travellers

My final words if India is safe for solo women or not is 'Yes', India is safe for women travelling alone provided that they take care of themselves. Although India is an extremely male dominated society and its misogynistic attitude towards women make it very hard for women not just for Indian women but also for female tourists to India. So, female travellers to India will need to be extra confident in their approach, be extremely savvy and be prepared to be incredibly assertive.

Basically, India is more or less a land of 'opportunities' where people take undue advantage and is not really an unsafe country. There are waiting opportunists at various points where travellers are most vulnerable such as near bazaars, railway stations, bus station, religious places etc.

Mind you, India is still a feudal and patriarchal society in many aspects. Despite its recent progress, there needs to be a generational change and shift in attitude. It will take another generation or perhaps two for attitudes to change and for society to allow healthy choices to its young men and women. We are aware that economic progress and development plays a huge role in creating a society that is modern in outlook and thinking. Today, large sections of Indian society are still unfortunately extremely poor by Western standards.

No matter where you are in India, do not isolate yourself or let anyone do it to you. You must remember to stay in busy places as they are less likely to be where people will try to harm you, at least physically. But unfortunately, busy places have always been places where terror attacks take place. Culprits and thugs are also present in crowded places to take undue advantage. In such situations, if you raise your voice, you'll be surprised how quickly they disappear. There are lots of people who will help out when in difficult situations. This means stay where the crowd is.

If you are going alone then make a point to go on tours with known and established operators. You must show confidence at all times and if you feel that someone or something is not right – just leave. There is no harm in offending anyone if you feel that a person might be a crook. At the end of the day, anyone who travels on their own have to be smart, be on the lookout and not do dangerous things or put themselves in dangerous situations.

I hope I have not been too negative and I sincerely hope you will visit India on your own. I have travelled alone in India and at times have felt scared at certain times but I have learnt that it's all about confidence and being careful. This is how most women who travel to India must be. Most Indians are like you and me and have similar concerns of safety as foreign travellers do. Indians are nice people and they will help you if required, some will even go that mile to help you out.

Message from the author

Thank you for reading my book. I request you to share that you've read my book on your Facebook, Twitter and/or LinkedIn accounts to spread the word about this book so that more women will be able to take advantage of the safety tips presented in this book.

If you want us to organise your trip to India then use the form here http://www.shalusharma.com/plan-your-trip and we can devise a customised travel plan for you.

I hope I've been helpful. If you need further advice or information, you can contact me from my website http://www.shalusharma.com or you can tweet me at https://twitter.com/bihar. You can always connect with me on Facebook. Don't hesitate to get in touch any time or ask a question. I will try my best to answer any questions that you might have.

Best wishes to you and have a nice and safe trip to India.

Take care

Shalu Sharma

References

Mark Magnier, June 2013. American tourist reportedly latest victim of rape in India: Los Angeles Times.

Foreigner Rape. 2013. NDTV.COM.

Two Western women raped in India: Irish charity worker, 21, 'drugged and assaulted' and U.S. hitchhiker, 30, gang-raped in resort town in separate attacks. June 2013. Mail Online.

Soutik Biswas, December 2013. How India treats its women. News India BBC.

UN Women in India. United Nations Entity for Gender Equality and the Empowerment of Women.

Kumar and Radhaa, 1993. The History of Doing: An Account of Women's Rights and Feminism in India.

Rape statistics around the world. September 2012. Indiatribune.com.

Bailable warrants against Katia. June 1998. Indian Express Newspapers.

Odisha ex-DGP's son Bitty Mohanty handed over to Rajasthan police. May 2013. The Indian Express.

Three held for raping Japanese tourists in Agra. September 2007. Indian Express

Pamela Timms, May 2008. Scarlett Keeling's diary reveals her sex, drink and drugs lifestyle. The Telegraph (UK)

Health Information for Travelers to India. Centers for Disease Control and Prevention.

Travellers, Travel Health Information Sheets. 2012. National Travel Health Network and Centre

Magnier et al, November 2008. India terrorist attacks leave at least 101 dead in Mumbai. Los Angeles Times.

Randeep Ramesh, May 2008. Series of six bomb blasts kills dozens in centre of Jaipur. The Guardian

Sheela Bhatt et al. July 2008. Serial blasts rock Ahmedabad. Rediff Abroad

Asseem Shaikh et al, February 2010. Blast rips Pune's German Bakery; 9 dead, 45 wounded. The Times of India.

Varanasi blast: Baby killed, Italian among 32 injured. December 2010. The Economic Times.

Shubham Ghosh, March 2013. Srinagar: Terror attack on CRPF camp, 2 terrorists killed. One India News.

Fifth Tourist Kidnapped in Kashmir. July 1995. The New York Times

Maoists kidnap two Italian tourists in India. March 2012. The Telegraph

Printed in Great Britain
by Amazon.co.uk, Ltd.,
Marston Gate.